The Ugly Sibling

The Drama of ANXIETY

James Ray Ashurst, Ph.D.

Cecil Yates, M.S.

BALBOA.PRESS

A DIVISION OF HAY HOUSE

Balboa Press books may be ordered through booksellers or by contacting:

Balboa Press
A Division of Hay House
1663 Liberty Drive
Bloomington, IN 47403
www.balboapress.com
844-682-1282

Because of the dynamic nature of the Internet, any web addresses or links contained in
this book may have changed since publication and may no longer be valid. The views
expressed in this work are solely those of the author and do not necessarily reflect the views
of the publisher, and the publisher hereby disclaims any responsibility for them.

The author of this book does not dispense medical advice or prescribe the use of any technique as a form of
treatment for physical, emotional, or medical problems without the advice of a physician, either directly or
indirectly. The intent of the author is only to offer information of a general nature to help you in your quest
for emotional and spiritual well-being. In the event you use any of the information in this book for yourself,
which is your constitutional right, the author and the publisher assume no responsibility for your actions.

Any people depicted in stock imagery provided by Getty Images are models,
and such images are being used for illustrative purposes only.
Certain stock imagery © Getty Images.

Scripture quotations marked KJV are from the Holy Bible, King James Version
(Authorized Version). First published in 1611. Quoted from the KJV Classic
Reference Bible, Copyright © 1983 by The Zondervan Corporation.

ISBN: 978-1-9822-6700-1 (sc)
ISBN: 978-1-9822-6699-8 (e)

Print information available on the last page.

Balboa Press rev. date: 04/07/2021

ACKNOWLEDGMENTS

Ms. Carolyn Baker—Proofreading the material

Ms. Joy Breedlove—Proofreading the material

This book is dedicated to the following:

Kelli Denning
Amy Grice

Their encouragement and guidance helped
make this book a reality.

CONTENTS

The three Ugly Siblings of stress, anxiety, and depression can immobilize an individual's life mentally, emotionally, socially, and physically. Many people throughout the world face these horrible illnesses each day, plus witnessing their impact on family members. These siblings can occupy the lives of children, teenagers, and adults.

Fortunately, these siblings are medically and psychologically treatable. There is amazing help available. This book provides useful ways of maintaining one's self-esteem, self-worth, and self-image while journeying through the corridors of the three siblings.

It is my wish that whether you suffer from any of the ugly siblings or not, this book will provide enlightenment and insights.

Anxiety is love's greatest killer.
--Anais Nin

CHAPTER 1
The Drama of Anxiety

THERE ARE THREE UGLY SIBLINGS that are inter-related with each other. The three are stress, anxiety, and depression (S.A.D.). Each has the potential to interrupt our daily functioning lives and create havoc. It is not unusual for each of us to experience some anxiety from time-to-time. It's quite normal and natural.

Our everyday situations can create circumstances that produce the anxiety. Anxiety is the worry or fear of what is about to take place or even what has already occurred. One may experience anxiety anywhere—at home, work, church, or school. If it becomes severe, it can definitely interfere with our daily activities.

Anxiety can happen when excessive worry takes over our lives. Common situations can activate our anxiety. Starting school, having to move away from loved ones, meeting a deadline, or paying bills are just a few situations that take our sunny day and place a dark cloud on it. While these may be serious at the moment, these normal cases of anxiety come and go within a specific amount of time. Usually they don't interfere with our daily functioning unless the anxiety becomes severe and mind-boggling. The three emotional bombardments can cause extreme havoc in one's life, and all three are related to one another. Each one individually can be extremely devastating, and they seem to have a personality of their own.

Each has the power to turn one's sunny, cheerful, and enthusiastic day into a horrible experience. The reason each can do so is due to the immense power that each is capable of enacting. And usually the three follow in the exact progression of a stressful life which eventually leads to anxious feelings, and then the devasting experience of depression.

Because of their destructive nature, I refer to them as the Three Ugly Siblings. They respect no persons since all ages can be inflicted with any of them. We can attempt to tackle each one at a time, but sometimes we sadly end up at the bottom of the emotional pile, gasping for breath.

Sooner or later we all experience the Three Siblings to some degree. Some of us face them when they are severe in our life. Some individuals are bombarded by them continuously. We long to get out of the clutches of the Ugly Three, but oh! It seems impossible. The Three can follow us everywhere, and we seem to be haunted by each one.

Since I have written books on stress and on depression, this book will focus on Anxiety. Which of the three is worse? Such an answer cannot be singled out because each can have a horrid impact of making a person's life miserable, disturbing, and even frightening. The fright can actually be paralyzing—just because one can't necessarily see stress, anxiety, or depression, we can certainly feel the chill, the impact, and their persona.

A crust eaten in peace is better than a
banquet partaken in anxiety.
--Aesop

CHAPTER 2
The Stressful Life

UGLY SIBLING #1

TO UNDERSTAND CLEARLY THE DYNAMICS of anxiety, one must comprehend the workings of stress in one's life. It is not simple by any means. Its complexity can be mind-boggling. Stress is appropriately called "the silent killer" because we do not know for certain how much destructive harm it is having on our physical, mental, and emotional selves. All three can be harmfully involved. No one is untouched—even children and teenagers. Nobody is shielded from this nasty "sibling" and even with the most perfect preventive means, usually, more than not, stress factors head full blast toward some degree of anxiety with a capital **A**. If no significant anxiety occurs after a bout of stress, you have been thoroughly blessed—almost unique.

He is truly great in power who has power over himself.
--Charles Spurgeon

Most of the information and dynamics concerning stress have been dealt with in my first book, **No-Nonsense Life Skills—Managing Your**

Stress. Our effective life skills can minimize our daily stressors in order that our lives can be more wholesome and less stressful. While there is no magic formula or magical wand to get rid of everyday problems and stress, all of us can apply certain lifestyles in order to lessen the second nasty "sibling" which is **anxiety**.

Stress by itself is a tremendous challenge to overcome. Mixing in anxiety, resulting from stress and depression can be more than one even bargained for during one's lifetime. We ask ourselves:

"What did I ever do to deserve this?"
"Is this the way my life is going to be?"
"What's the answer and where must I go?

It isn't that anxiety is not a normal and healthy feeling at times because it can givs us clear and concise warning that something might be amiss in one's life. It is wise to "listen" to such emotion.

No one can make you feel inferior without your consent.
---Eleanor Roosevelt

However, on the flip side of the healthy side of anxiety are unhealthy anxious moments that can cause physical, mental, and emotional problems. The third ugly sibling that goes with stress and anxiety is depression:

Stress=S

Anxiety=A

Depression=D

When the three ugly siblings are in full force, it can indeed be a very SAD day for the individual.

When an individual's anxiety carries with it excessive nervousness, fear, and emotional worry, then the ugly sibling is taking on a different character than a healthy anxiety.

WATCH OUT!!

Trust God. You are exactly where you are meant to be.
---Hallmark

CHAPTER 3
Esther: If I Perish, I Perish.

THERE ARE MANY STORIES ABOUT Biblical heroes and heroines who God has used in His plans and purposes over the history of mankind. These persons, though relying in faith upon God, have made or caused great impact upon other persons, groups, and nations, and they have caused small and great changes in human history. Esther, a young Jewish maiden, remains one of these. The period of time was around 520–510 B.C.

The Jewish nation had been taken captive and dispersed over 120 provinces of Persia. Many of the Jewish people were living in the area of Shushan, the location of the king who was very rich and powerful.

After reigning for 3 years, King Ahasueras wished to display the splendor and glory of his regime, and he invited nobles, princes, and servants to Shushan. There were great festivities. The king ordered Vashti, the queen, to make an appearance so all could see her beauty. She refused the king's request to become a public display. This was a terribly embarrassing matter to the king and all those in attendance. By royal order, Vashti "could come no longer before the king" so her royal estate was to be given to another. Letters were sent out to all the provinces that "every man should bear rule in his own house." This became the law of the land.

In the absence of Queen Vashti, servants of the king recommended "fair young maidens" be sought throughout the kingdom and brought into the Sushan castle for the king. The maiden who pleased the king the most would become the new queen. She would receive the entire estate that had once belonged to Vashti.

Living in Shushan was a godly Jewish man named Mordecai, a Benjamite, who had been carried away from Israel through the captivity. He took into his care a young maiden, his niece, named **"Hadassah, that is, Esther"**, whose parents had died. She was young, fair, and beautiful. Esther, along with others, was brought into the house of the King. These maidens went through a process of twelve months of purification before each one in turn was to "go in to the king". Of the many maidens, the king loved Esther above all the other women. Esther obtained grace and favor in the eyes of the king. Vashti was out.

Sitting near the gate to the castle was Mordecai who overheard two of the king's chamberlains plotting to take the king's life. Mordecai made it known to Queen Esther who then made it known to the king. The two men were caught, tried, and later hanged. Mordecai's actions would later be recognized and be richly rewarded.

Also located in Shushan was a very ungodly and evil man named Haman. He was promoted to a very high and influential position in the government. He developed an intense ambition of becoming as powerful and authoritative as that of the king. He began requiring citizens to bow to him when in his presence. Mordecai neither bowed not showed any respect for Haman. Haman became furious and had a scaffold erected to hang Mordecai,

Haman was informed that Mordecai was a Jew and that there were many Jews scattered across the kingdom who had laws different from those of the kingdom. He requested that the king decree to destroy all these individuals within the provinces.

Mordecai learned of this plan and sent word to Esther as to the situation. The Bible tells that Esther was **"exceedingly grieved."** Historically, this term implied "harassment, oppression, vexation, affliction and distress of mind." Esther was under the greatest pressure and anxiety in her life. Not only was her own life at stake, but the life of Mordecai and the lives of millions of Jews scattered over Persian provinces. This was a critical point in the lives of all Jewish people, resting upon the decision of the young Jewish Queen.

Esther began to consider the matter thoroughly and determined not only to rely upon her faith in God, but to take decisive action on her own toward saving her people. She made the intelligent decision to seek advice from Mordecai.

Mordecai advised her to go to the king and make supplication for her people's survival. Esther recognized great danger for herself in doing so. Should an "uncalled visitor" go unto the king, that person faced death unless the king should "hold out the golden scepter that the person might live." Should the king not hold out the golden scepter to Esther, she would be killed, and every person within the Jewish Nation would be sought out and killed. Great pressure was upon Esther.

Esther replied to Mordecai's warning: **I will go in unto the king, which is not according to the law: and if I perish, I perish" – Esther 4:16.** Esther requested Mordecai to see that all Jews pray and fast for three days. Esther decided to go in unto the king and make supplication on behalf of herself and the Jews.

On the third day, Esther stood in the inner court of the king's house. When the king saw Esther, **"she obtained favour in the king's sight: and the king held out the golden scepter. So Esther drew near, and touched the top of the scepter in his hand."** She requested the king and Haman attend a banquet that she would prepare for them.

The king and Haman attended the banquet the following day. It was there that the king was informed by Esther about the plot to eliminate all Jews, including Mordecai and Esther. The king asked by whom and where is the person who had ordered this. Esther answered, **"The adversary and enemy is this wicked Haman."** The king became extremely angry and left the banquet. Upon the king's command, Haman was taken to his own built gallows and hanged. Additionally, Haman's sons were also hanged on the gallows.

The king, being reminded that it was Mordecai who had previously saved his life, gave his royal ring to Mordecai. The ring gave him full power and authority in the position second only to the king. Mordecai was instructed to write a decree to the entire kingdom that protected the Jewish people against all who would attempt to harm them. Mordecai then went out from the king, dressed in royal apparel, and **"wearing a garment of fine linen and purple"** as the city of Shushan rejoiced.

"The Jews had light, and gladness, and joy, and honour"—Esther 8:17

God may allow pressures and anxieties to be placed upon us in order to accomplish a part of His divine plan for us and others. The person He uses in such a case may not know or appreciate the face that he is being used and possibly promoted in life for God's own divine reasons. One must always accept that such a case may exist when he or she experiences great anxieties under worldly pressures.

Consider what a young Jewish maiden accomplished by trusting in God and following Godly advice when placed under the greatest of anxiety and pressures. Esther became the queen of the largest and most powerful kingdom on earth at the time. She made a godly decision that saved her life, the life of her uncle, and the life of the Nation Israel in captivity. She became a heroine to her people, the Jews. A two-day celebration called Purim was initiated and is still revered and observed by Jews. She will always be remembered as the young maiden who under great stress and anxieties made the correct, righteous, and timely decision, **"If I perish, I perish."**

CHAPTER 4
The Symptoms Of Anxiety

UGLY SIBLING #2

THERE ARE MANY SYMPTOMS OF the anxiety disorder or severe "sibling anxiety" while some overlap the normal sense of anxiety. When one knows that one's life is totally chaotic, it is probably the acute anxiety. Some of the symptoms are as follows:

* **High blood pressure—Over a long period of time, this can lead to harmful health conditions.**

* **Restlessness—This is frustrating because the body will not allow the person to relax and to rest.**

* **Insomnia—The body needs and craves sleep. Without adequate amount, the body has a difficult time functioning with life responsibilities.**

* **Concentration on problems—This is highly frustrating because the problems need some type of solution so that life can return to a normal state of mind.**

* **Irritability—This goes way beyond what is our normal irritability in life. This creates increased anger and frustration,**

and the more that things don't go right, the worse the emotions get.

★ **Worry--All of us worry from time-to-time about situations and people in our lives. However, this worry is obsessive and can create psychological problems that prevent the individual from performing his or her home and work responsibilities.**

★ **Sadness—This is not the normal brand of being sad over a life situation. This sadness is intertwined with one's anxiety over what is happening in their life at the time. Because we are all different folks, we will not experience the same symptoms as someone else in our friend circle.**

While there are different anxiety disorders, the most common one is Generalized Anxiety Disorder. The individual finds himself or herself worried or fretted about nonspecific life events and objects. The individual cannot always identify the cause of the anxiety. It's just there! This anxiety disorder never lets up on the person. You fight it continually, but for the most time, it wins the battle between you and whatever is worrying you at the time. The highly frustrating dilemma is that the person doesn't have the slightest idea of where the generalized anxiety is coming from. This ugly Sibling plans on keeping it a secret.

Not everyone who has a generalized anxiety disorder has the next type of anxiety disorder called a Panic Attack. These attacks are sudden and usually brief characterized by intense terror and fear. These horrid attacks escalate quickly, usually without any warning, and leave the individual almost paralyzed at the time. They are so very scary and frightening, the individual has the instant urge to leave where they are and find a safe place to "hide out", to locate peace and security. Sometimes, that place is located in a local hospital. During the panic attack, the victim may actually thinking he or she is having a heart attack or a stroke. At such a point, the individual's panic attack is enhanced, which creates more fear and anxiety. By the time the person reaches the hospital, he or she is a nervous wreck. After the hospital doctors do their tests and procedures, the diagnosis is not a heart attack or a stroke but a full-blown panic (anxiety) attack. While such news will sound comforting to the victim, the anxiety attack still has to be dealt with.

While most panic attacks last for only a brief time, they seem much longer. So as to not get trapped by one of the attacks at an event, some individuals will sit on the end of a row of seats to "run" for safety in case of an attack. If no end seat is available, the person will choose to stand or to simply leave the situation because one never knows what will trigger the attack. It remains a mystery!

The first panic attack a friend told us about happened to him at a college football game. It was during the third quarter. He wasn't sure what was going on in his body. It happened suddenly—no warning whatsoever. Just WHAM! He could hardly catch his breath, and the sweating and coolness covered his body. He felt the urgent need to leave the stadium.

After telling his friends that he was ill, he headed to the campus infirmary. It was a long walk. By the time the infirmary came into sight, our friend was shaking from head to toe, worried out of his mind. His fear and anxiety brought many possible illnesses to his mind. The tingling subsided as the medication took effect, but he still needed answers. As the weeks passed, our friend acquainted himself with the drama of anxiety attacks. This was a smart move on his part since he has had several panic attacks since his first one.

Immediately before the attack, a person may feel a chill or even a hot flash cover one's body. It's a feeling that won't ever be forgotten. Several symptoms may follow the chills or hot flashes:

* **shortness of breath**
* **sweating**
* **worry/fear**
* **distress**
* **tingling**

All of these, and more, result from being anxious about someone (Social Anxiety Disorder), being separated from a loved one (Separation Anxiety Disorder), or some situation (Generalized Anxiety Disorder). The sadness is that anxiety has so many symptoms and causes.

Anxiety is the rust of life, destroying its brightness and weakening its power.
--Tyron Edwards

CHAPTER 5
Disciples In The Storm

HERE ARE MANY STORIES IN the Bible concerning individuals finding themselves in stressful events, each serving as an example of individuals dealing with the anxieties of life. Each event provides opportunity to utilize our faith in God's Word. Hence, these events become spiritual tests to reflect the quality of our faith in God and His Word as we live out our lives. We are each in the process of teaching individuals the power of spiritual living.

One of the Bible stories of individuals having great anxiety, pressure, and fear is the story of Jesus' disciples in the storm—Matthew 8:23-27. The disciples had been "students" of Jesus for some time and were well informed about who He was and His purpose on earth. The greater the knowledge of God's Word in our memory bank, the greater the spiritual solutions to deal with the problems of life.

Adversity in each believer's life is designed for blessing and to teach each of us the futility of human resources and the necessity of trusting God and His Word. Every storm of life provides the opportunity for the believer to apply the content of his spiritual knowledge to the situation.

The stormy sea in Matthew represents the variable circumstances of life, including everything from the calm to the storm. One's spiritual life is neutralized by fear and anxiety. When this occurs, one becomes afraid in life and a slave to circumstances and thereby suffers under self-induced misery.

As the anxiety-stricken disciples came to wake the sleeping Lord, their eyes were upon the storm. Their focus was not on the Lord. They were reacting to the storm, not trusting in the Lord. There was no atmosphere of divine strength displayed in the actions of the disciples. They had forgotten that it was Jesus' humanity that was asleep with His Deity in the process of holding the entire universe together. The ship could not sink with Him onboard. They had forgotten who Jesus was and had also forgotten that God had a divine plan for each one's future life. To be on the ship at that moment was the safest place in the universe. The disciples would learn much from their failure to deal with this storm. The disciples were in a horrifying emotional state of anxiety. They were beset with a terrible load of fear. Fear was controlling their lives.

While Jesus was asleep, He was illustrating to the disciples the concept of "faith-rest" that He had previously taught them. He was at perfect peace with Himself during the storm. He was providing each disciple the privacy and privilege to apply the actual power of God through their lives in this event. Hence, they had the freedom to utilize what they had been taught or to try to handle this experience through human wisdom. They failed. We each must decide which is more real—**the circumstances we face or God's Word in the human soul.**

Jesus reprimanded the disciples before He calmed the wind and sea. Why? The class being taught was not over. It was still in session. The storm was not the issue. The issue was the disciples' lack of faith in God's Word:

And he saith unto them, Why are ye fearful, O ye of little faith? Then he arose, and rebuked the winds and the sea; and there was a great calm.

The "great calm" that followed this event is of special interest. We should be aware that as we apply God's Word to our own storms today, we can and will experience great peace of mind and a great calmness of the soul. This is the Christian life.

CHAPTER 6
Dealing With Anxiety

ANXIETY DISORDERS ARE COMPLICATED BECAUSE many might take place at the same time or one anxiety might well trigger another different one. One cause of anxiety might originate from our personal environment, such as school life, work stressors, family difficulties, and yes! even in our relationship with others. One can well have multi-anxiety difficulties at the same time.

Some researchers believe that genetics can play a role in others in the family displaying similar anxiety problems. For some individuals over a certain age, medical situations, surgeries, and medications seem a way of life—these can cause tremendous anxiety problems.

> **Do not regret growing older...**
> **It's a privilege denied to many.**
> --anonymous

There are ways to prevent or even reduce the risk of anxiety emotions:

A great deal of research has been transacted on anxiety and the various ways to reduce the symptoms. One way is to cut back on one's intake of caffeine. Coffee drinkers, relax! The research doesn't promote getting rid of all the caffeine but rather to reduce the amount one drinks.

Maintaining a healthy diet is yet another means of reducing one's stress and anxiety levels. In our society where "fast food" has become our way of life, we fail to keep a healthy diet plan. We wander off the trail, and this creates havoc with our bodily system.

An irregular sleep pattern will definitely awaken "the beast" in us. All of us have probably had those sleepless nights in which our eyelids hadn't secured enough sleep. And the longer I stayed in bed…and awake, the madder I became with myself—(a no win situation)—The madder I became, the longer I stayed awake. Sleep is a necessary ingredient for the human body, but it must be on a regular pattern. Go to bed at a certain time and arise at a certain time.

A fourth treatment is to avoid or reduce alcoholic drinks. Alcohol is a depressant in our system. It invites anxiety problems into our lives, so the individual not only has the emotions of fear, worry, and anxiety but an element of a depressant which makes life's situations seem worse. Thus, the individual takes out his or her anxieties on family members, friends, and personnel at work.

The last treatment is a MUST. Avoid recreational drugs. Such drugs mess with one's mental and emotional state of being. Hallucinations can develop with bizarre behavior. The drugs put the individual into a heightened state where anxieties, fear, and worry have the freedom to invade the mind. In addition, when one is coming down from the particular drug, havoc and chaos become partners in creating a mental and emotional nightmare.

Because anxiety problems are so prevalent in our society today, treatments have been established to help individuals cope with their anxiety. Due to the anxiety problems in the workplace, in family matters, and throughout our society, individuals are inundated with the drama of fear, worry, and anxiety. We try to escape by finding solutions, but we are surrounded by the enemy (anxiety).

"How Can I Cope?"

"Am I going crazy?"

"What's normal anymore?"

These questions and more penetrate our minds. We seek to understand our personal anxieties which motivates us to get help from the medical profession. The answer to our anxiety problems is relatively simple: treat yourself with love and kindness and intelligence. When we view the list below, we will notice that the treatment involves placing ourselves as priority! We don't sit in the "back seat" but rather in the "front seat" of life. The idea of everyone else coming first is a disastrous concept. We cannot give to others what we ourselves don't have. We cannot attack our anxious situations successfully unless we are physically, mentally, and emotionally in good shape.

When we begin to live the list of treatment into our lives, we will begin to notice a marvelous change, Anxieties don't all of a sudden dissolve, but they do begin to lose their power in our lives because we are physically, mentally, and emotionally fit to face them effectively. We'll be able to Stand Our Ground against ugly sibling #2. You will have the inner power to combat the anxieties with confidence and understanding.

* **Seek professional therapy—there is no shame in getting help.**
* **Medication—ask your physician for assistance.**
* **Make lifestyle changes—take care of your body.**
* **Participate in healthy activities, use common sense.**
* **Eliminate unhealthy activities with negative impact.**
* **Use meditation techniques—this requires quiet time.**

* **Stay active, exercise or just walk.**
* **Exercise—join a gym.**

Some of these may be difficult to do; however, starting is the key. For the sake of your body and sanity, start somewhere!

RISKS! RISKS! RISKS!

Being anxious about a situation or person creates a certain degree of worry. However, anxious behavior doesn't end there. Anxiety can stir up more problems than any one of us would want to handle. The anxious worry can create bouts of depression, along with stress. It is not uncommon for a stressed person with a problem to begin misusing substances (recreational drugs and alcohol). Such misuse leads to more problems. No matter how hard one tries, the substance misuses bring more stress. anxiety, and even depression.

Because the anxiety presents problems functioning at work, at home, and in the social arena, we simply aren't ourselves because the anxious moments take over and leave us "lost" in our world. We may experience "social isolation" in which people avoid having much to do with us. We can feel the isolation. Our anxiety is so powerful that others will choose to go the other way when they see us coming.

Living an anxious lifestyle robs the individual of a wonderful quality of life. It is impossible to enjoy life when one operates his or her mind on consistent anxious moments.

Every tomorrow has two handles. We can take hold of it by the handle of anxiety or by the handle of faith.
---anonymous

CHAPTER 7
The Rope Of Scarlet Thread

ONE OF THE GREATEST STORIES of the Bible is found in the first few chapters of the Book of Joshua. It is the story of Rahab, a harlot who lived in the city of Jericho, a walled city, just to the east of the Jordan River. The story occurred during a very evil period of time in that part of the world, around 1450 BC. Nations in that area were encumbered with horrors of Baal worship and human sacrifices. One of the worst forms of this worship was found in Jericho.

The Book of Joshua concerns the people of Israel having left their bondage in Egypt and traveling for over 40 years as a nation of God's choosing to move toward their homeland. During this period, God was generating events of evangelism for the entire world. People of all nations had become aware of the failure of Egypt's Pharaoh in pursuing the Jewish people. Significant events were generated by God for the people of Israel to show the world that they were "the people of God" and that He was empowering them under His divine protection. God was sending the message to the world that Israel was His own nation of people. The Hebrew people had moved to a point just across the Jordan River. Through God's power, they had won victory after victory against ungodly cities, kings, and nations. The next movement would be to cross River Jordan into Canaan and prepare for battle to take the land. The land was then occupied by cities and groups of very ungodly people. The Hebrews were instructed by God to drive out or destroy everyone and take possession of the entire land. The first city the Israelites would encounter with this mission would be Jericho.

The inhabitants of Jericho were aware that when Israel attacked this walled city, they would all be destroyed. After the destruction, the entire city and everything within the walls would be burned out of existence. The great wall surrounding the city would first be destroyed by God.

History records the vicious nature of a branch of Baal worship in that part of the world called the Baal Melquart worship system. This system was alive in Jericho. In horror during worship events, victims were thrown alive as sacrifices into festival bonfires, including unwanted spouses, children, and others who did not fit sufficiently within their ungodly culture. The firstborn male child of each king was sacrificed by being placed alive in sealed hollows of stone gate pillars. This evil culture was more than sufficient reason for the destruction of Jericho by God.

Within the walls of Jericho, anxiety was rampant among all the people. Fear was now at its greatest level because the Hebrews were located just across the Jordan River. The harlot, Rahab, was among those who was fearful and stated **"Our heart did melt, neither did anymore courage remain in any. Terror is fallen upon us."** We cannot imagine the anxiety Rahab possessed at that point in time. She was living in a state of personal terror. It appeared that she and her family were about to be totally destroyed, along with the entire city's population.

While terrorized people of Jericho awaited their fate, Joshua was providing instructions and guidance to the Hebrew nation concerning plans for the imminent attack. He sent out 2 spies to search the land, the people, and the city of Jericho, and then to report back their findings. The 2 spies entered Jericho and **"came into a harlot's house, named Rahab, and lodged there."** The king of the city was told of this, had an inquiry made, and ordered Rahab to "bring forth" the 2 men. Rahab defied the order, hid the 2 spies on the roof of her house under stalks of flax and informed the king that the two men had left the city at the fall of darkness.

If the king had suspected Rahab was not telling the truth, Rahab would certainly have been put to death. She had put herself and the 2 spies at great risk. The tension in her life had to be at a greater point than at any other time in her life. She was facing the possibility of death. She was also facing the fact of her being put to death along with the members of her family in the coming invasion from the Hebrews. She had 2 spies from the approaching Hebrews on her hands. All this was cause for great anxiety, fear, and terror of heart.

In the midst of these great pressures, Rahab possessed a heart of great discernment that others in Jericho did not possess. She had heard of the greatness and power of the God of the Hebrews and believed in Him (Josh. 2:11). She had become a believer in the Lord God of Israel and recognized His divine power prior to her encounter with the spies.

To provide a means of escape for the two spies, she tied a **"rope of scarlet thread"** to a window to allow the men to get down the wall in the dark. For this, she asked a promise of safety for herself and her family. The spies agreed. The scarlet rope hanging from the window would be a "token" of their promise of delivering her and her family. Binding the rope to the window was an action of faith on her part. The rope was a visible marker of her faith in the spies, their oath to her, the Hebrew nation, and now to her God. It was a divine promise that became her divine hope for future deliverance from destruction. Her anxiety, fears, and terror were gone!

As Rahab bound the **'line of scarlet thread"** to the window, she was in faith trusting God for her deliverance as well as deliverance of her family members. It was guaranteed. She had turned the matter over to God. She was relaxed and at perfect peace within. Her sense of terror was no more.

The Hebrew attack on the city of Jericho came to pass with total destruction, including the formidable walls crumbing under the power of God. Only the house of Rahab sheltering her family survived. She and her family were moved away from Jericho to follow the Hebrews. After a period of time, they were allowed into the encampment of Israel and accepted as part of the community.

As a special honor, Rahab was entered by God into the Hebrew family and the linage of King David and the person of Jesus Christ. Scarlet, the color of blood. We see scarlet as the color representing Christ's work on the cross. His shed blood. We see in this representation of Christ's death, burial, and resurrection, the very hope for our future. Today our "scarlet rope" is the Holy Bible. It is our "token" and absolute "surety of God's promises" that provides for our present as well as for our future.

CHAPTER 8
Nightmare!

IT WAS A PICTURE PERFECT spring day. The soft breeze felt great, and the cool temperature made Jason's outing to the local park with his Beagle, Rascal, absolutely ideal. Very few individuals had taken the same opportunity, so for the most part, the park belonged to Jason.

Rascal's favorite game was chasing the soft, red rubber ball that Jason would throw towards the various landmarks located in the small community park. Jason had no idea when he arrived at the park what a nightmare he would encounter that gorgeous spring afternoon.

Jason was feeling in excellent shape. After all, he was young and in good health. The tragedy occurred without any warning. Jason and Rascal had been playing "fetch the ball" for 45 minutes when Jason felt an unusual tingling slowly move across his body. He had never before experienced such a strange sensation.

Jason had been in excellent health and shape. As sweat broke out on his body, he felt he was having a heart attack or maybe a stroke. Panic and anxiety encompassed his whole being. Rascal was staying a good distance away from her master. She knew something was very wrong.

Jason's throat became extremely tight, causing problems in breathing. His body was shaking uncontrollably to a point of feeling dizzy. While this was going on, Jason's friend, Barbara and her dog, happened on the scene. Being a nurse, she knew what Jason was experiencing.

"Jason, sit down."

"Now take some slow breaths. Take in several and hold them and then slowly let them out."

Barbara knew to stay calm as she gave out her instructions to Jason.

"Barbara, what's going on with me?"

"Jason, you are having a panic attack and a very bad one."

"Barbara, I feel like I'm coming apart. It's like I am having a nightmare."

"Jason, that's a normal feeling. You are not alone. I'm here with you until it passes."

"How long will it take?"

"Each attack is different, but just remain calm and still. Think about a pleasant scenery or memory."

Before long, Jason's body became totally relaxed. The panic attack had passed.

"Jason, if you ever have another one, just recall what I've told you."

"You bet I will!"

Barbara could tell that Jason was in a recovery state of mind because he was throwing Rascal's ball towards the wide-open field.

CHAPTER 9
The Burning Bush Episode

GREAT HEROES OF THE BIBLE were often confronted with events that created tremendous anxiety and fear. They were not immune from these occasions and from the anxiety and panic they brought out. The burning bush in Exodus 3-4 was brought upon Moses to prepare him for use by God in delivering the Hebrews from bondage in Egypt to their homeland.

Moses was in the process of keeping his father-in-law's sheep in the area of Midian. He observed a bush burning in the distance that was not being consumed—a true sight of wonder! As he approached the site, the voice of God spoke to him, from the bush, identifying himself as **"I am."** Moses was told to take off his shoes for the ground upon which he stood was "holy ground."

It is difficult to imagine the intensity of the anxiety and fear of Moses at this moment in time. Nothing had ever prepared him for such a significant event—being confronted in person by God, the creator of the universe. For Moses, it was a moment of fear and anxiety. The pressure was tremendous. In a sense, Moses "fainted" in the situation—he became overwhelmed with the fear and panic. We, too, presently live in an age when individuals faint during periods of great pressure and anxiety.

It was beyond the imagination of Moses to comprehend what this situation was all about. Moses' interest was focused upon the burning bush and the one-on-one personal presence of Almighty God. While Moses' focus was upon the event, God had a major and historically significant purpose for the visit. This story presents the problem of one who focuses upon a pressured situation as a crisis without realizing there is often a great and divine purpose of God in allowing such events to come our way. We should always continue to put our trust in God and His Word for divine resolution to each crisis we face.

The impact of the burning bush event would set into motion what God could and would do through Moses for the rest of his life. Many opportunities would be presented to Moses for God to demonstrate His power to the rest of the world, including a diversity of marvelous events during the deliverance of the Hebrews from Egyptian bondage.

Following the burning bush encounter, God issued guidelines for Moses. God provided details as to what Moses was to do and how and when to do it. Moses, after arguing with God about his lack of skills and ability, set out to follow God's detailed instructions. We may view ourselves, like Moses, as having a lack of skills, knowledge or know-how to successfully get through crises and how to know what to do or say in many situations. The issue for each of us is knowing what God has to say to us through His Word.

Each crisis has the characteristics of testing. Similar to physically exercising, building up the muscles in our bodies, testing makes our spiritual muscles strong. The more tests and greater the weight, the stronger we become in God. It takes continual testing to maintain the capacity for God to utilize His spiritual power and strength through our lives. Thus, we can expect God to continue to allow each of us to face trials and problems in the development of our spiritual lives. Problems creating anxiety that come our way test us to determine if we will fall apart, get upset, get disturbed, or become totally disoriented. Thus, we need to teach ourselves to depend upon God for everything in all occasions—good, bad, or indifferent.

As we continue daily to depend upon God and His Word, we begin to become clearer thinkers. We enter a "field of rest." We can remain there during periods and times of unrest in the circumstances we find ourselves. If we do so, there will come a peace and understanding which will cause us to be ready for the crisis when it comes. "What is God trying to do with me in this situation?" If we begin to think spiritually, we will be able to follow through on these occasions. We will be able to stand in the crises and successfully mix our knowledge of God's Word with His promises and live in true spiritual faith.

On a daily and consistent basis, we should know, understand, and trust in God's promise **"that all things work together for good to them who love God, to them who are the called according to his purpose— Romans 8:28."** This is living by divine viewpoint and is pleasing to God. As we develop and live with this divine lifestyle of personal peace, God will be able to use us in His ongoing plans. We should always remain aware of the promise, **"For God hath not given us the spirit of fear; but of power and of love, and of a sound mind—II Timothy 1:7."**

It is interesting that during Moses' confrontation with God that God was persistent in providing Moses with promises as to what and how Moses could be used to deliver Israel from Egypt. Moses was finally convinced that the deliverance of Israel did not depend upon himself but upon the plan and the power of God. Moses had to totally depend upon the promises God had provided him at the burning bush. For the power of God to take place and to be effective, Moses had to trust God and follow His divine instructions.

Moses took God at His Word and began to follow through with the divine plan to deliver Israel. Moses confronted Pharaoh and told him that God had said, "Let my people go." Pharaoh refused, and Egypt began to suffer greatly through various plagues. Finally being allowed to leave, the Hebrews began their journey toward their homeland.

The Israelites' journey home required 40 tough years under Moses' leadership and God's direction. There were times when anxiety appeared among the people as to whether they would reach their homeland. However, through Moses' submission to God's instructions, he became the most powerful figure of that period of history.

There are lessons one can learn in studying the Biblical account of "the exodus" story. There are always a bigger story and a greater purpose behind crises and anxieties we face. We can, like Moses, come to trust the Lord and His Word in difficult situations in life and **"stand still and see the deliverance of the Lord."** God is certainly able to take care of each of us because He has a wonderful plan for each of our lives.

CHAPTER 10
From Bittnerss To Joy

THE STORY OF NAOMI AND Ruth occurred around the period 1322 B.C. to 1312 B. C., an era when the judges ruled Israel and the Mosaic Law was of great importance. There had been a period of great famine in the land of Israel in which everyone had been impacted. One of the righteous citizens living in Bethlehem left with his family to go to Moab, a country just to the east of the Jordan River. It was a matter of family survival for Elimelech, his wife Naomi, and their two sons.

After arriving in Moab, Elimelech soon died, followed by the deaths of the two sons. However, the sons had each married a wife of Moab heritage, Orpah and Ruth. For a period of time, the three women lived together caring and supporting each other. Both daughters-in-law loved Naomi and strived to care for her. There was not a caretaker for the women and no source of income for their survival in Moab. The country was not a friendly place for Naomi who was a Jew, nor for either of the two daughters. Moab was filled with Baal worship, an anathema for Naomi, who was a righteous Jew. Naomi made the decision to return to Bethlehem as there was information that Israel was now prospering and food was plentiful. Naomi also had relatives still living in the area of Bethlehem.

Soon after departing on the journey, Naomi stopped with the two daughters-in-law and advised them to return each to their mother's house. Each wept at the thought of separation from Naomi. Orpah decided to return to her mother's house while Ruth remained with Naomi.

Ruth realized something that Orpah failed to see. Ruth's association with Naomi had led her to see there was only one supreme God. She also realized that she had much more to learn about the true spiritual life she needed. Her personal sense of values caused her to appreciate what she saw in the integrity of Naomi. Even though she chose to stay with Naomi, Ruth knew of the difficulties she may encounter by being a Moabitess who had become a Jew. She would remain with Naomi and go with her to Bethlehem. This was a historical decision that would change her life and the lives of others forever.

After crossing the Jordan River and traveling half-way across Israel, the two women arrived in Bethlehem. All the city asked, "Is this Naomi?" She said to them, "Call me not Naomi, call me Mara because God has dealt very bitterly with me." Ruth and Naomi had been brought very closely together as a result of their struggling with anxiety, fear, and the bitterness of life they had confronted.

The term "Mara" expressed by Naomi means "Soldiers of the army of the evil one or Angels of Evil." This was a term describing a person being absolute destitute of any sense of good or worth. This was also an expression of bitterness. Both Naomi and Ruth had reached the point of sensing that God had done them wrong and had taken away everything and everyone of importance. It appeared that their lives were hopeless and without any godly support. They were without a source of income or livelihood. Now, they had returned penniless to Bethlehem in a state of destitution and hopelessness.

Behind this desperate situation, God was preparing to use both women in a mighty way in fulfilling a vital step in His planning and revelation to bring forth a Divine Redeemer for Ruth, Naomi, and the entire human race.

Ruth and Naomi moved back into the house vacated by the family of Naomi when they left years ago to go to Moab. Needing food, Ruth went into the countryside to glean leftovers from grain harvesting, a very slow and tiresome task. She was noticed by the owner of the land, a man whose name was Boaz, who inquired of the regular workers as to her identity. He was told she was Ruth, the daughter-in-law of Naomi. He told workers to allow her to glean and to assist by leaving extra grain behind for her to pick up and take home. Ruth told Naomi about the event. Naomi revealed to her that Boaz was a near kinsman of the family.

It was toward the end of the harvest season and time for seasonal festivities and celebration of the harvest. The men would eat and drink, and then lie down to sleep on the harvest floor. According to Jewish custom and Mosaic Law, Naomi instructed Ruth to observe the location that Boaz would like down to sleep and then to lie down at his feet, pulling his cloak over her feet. As Ruth did so, Boaz awakened and told Ruth for to leave before others awakened and that he would do the part of a kinsman. The next day, Boaz went up to the gate and held a public meeting with ten witnesses that he desired to redeem or purchase the land Naomi had to sell as well as the land of Ruth's former husband, the son of Naomi. Boaz did so, as all this was according to Mosaic Law. Only a near relative, a kinsman, could purchase or redeem the land of a Jew. The land is to be kept in the hands of the same family.

Soon Boaz took Ruth as his wife. She bore a son. Great relief and happiness had arrived at last. The bitterness of life had been replaced by godly joy for Naomi and Ruth. Boaz and Ruth named their son Obed.

Obed became the father of Jesse who became the father of David, the King of Israel.

Boaz was a man used by God to perform the duty of a Redeemer. He possessed a great and virtuous character. Boaz fulfilled all four of the Biblical requirements to be a redeemer, just as Jesus Christ fulfilled them on behalf of the human race.

The four requirements are as follows:

* ★ *He must be a kinsman to redeem.*
* ★ *He must be willing to redeem.*
* ★ *He must be able to redeem.*
* ★ *He must take action to redeem.*

CHAPTER 11

Depression

UGLY SIBLING #3

THE THIRD UGLY SIBLING THAT can occur due to a tremendous amount of stress and overwhelming anxiety is **depression.** At times, our daily life experiences sadness, gloominess, moodiness, misery, and depression. Depression is an illness that can be terrifying and paralyzing, sometimes leading to suicidal thoughts or even to suicide itself. There is no vaccine to prevent it, thus making it a scary and horrific illness with the power to destroy a person's livelihood and positive outlook on life.

Depressed people can quickly fall out of a love for life; their existence is an hourly struggle on some days, especially around holidays. The factors of a depressive state can rob a person of joy, happiness, and genuine relaxation. This ugly sibling can destroy a fulfilling life of contentment, pleasure, and well-being, and its impact can be on adults, teenagers, and children. In addition, it can create havoc in personal relationships among family members and close friends.

Unless you've had depression, I don't thank you're qualified to talk about it.

---Geoffrey Boycott

This ugly sibling does have symptoms by which a person can be impacted. Some are as follows:

a. **Listlessness**—lacking energy and enthusiasm, being lethargic about everything.

b. **Inability to relax**—experiencing anxiety, jitteriness, impatience, and tension.

c. **Total fatigue**—chronic tiredness, wishing to sleep a great deal.

d. **Sadness, despondency, despair, and loneliness**—these make life seem deplorable.

e. **Significant changes in appetite**—gaining or losing weight.

f. **Dark mood**—a gloomy and sulky state of mind.

g. **Hopelessness**—feeling that life is without purpose.

h. **Inability to concentrate, focus, or make simple decisions**—mind is distracted.

i. **Lack of sociability**—avoiding friends and family members.

j. **Recurring thoughts of suicide and death.**

This ugly sibling can make each day a tremendous challenge. Just getting out of bed can be totally gut-wrenching. Depressed persons can be good at hiding their illness at times because they are either embarrassed or afraid of what people will say or think.

A depressed person's thinking is often distorted, unrealistic, and fragmented. The victim may certainly mean well, but their thinking is cloudy and without true merit. A depressed person is not trying to be argumentative and unclear; it's the illness that is in control.

The lifestyle of a depressed person is hard for one to imagine who has never experienced such a grotesque illness. Depressed people exist in a complex world. They may experience extreme humiliation and shame for being a "victim" of the complex illness. They may even shy away from divulging their disease.

What makes depression such a draining illness is that every single day and night is a tremendous challenge. Who is going to win? The depression or you? If the depression wins, then the individual will definitely be exhausted at the close of the day with no energy left. Depressed people long to rest, sleep, nap, lounge, and plainly flop down. It isn't because they're lazy—far from it. They are simply out of gas for the day; they have absolutely no get-up-and-go to complete the rest of the indoor and outdoor household chores, which leads to stress, anxiety, frustration, and anger.

Depression remains one of the greatest unsolved medical mysteries.
---Anne Sheffield

CONCLUSION

HE THREE UGLY SIBLINGS OF stress, anxiety, and depression can create destruction in a person's functioning life. In fact, each solitary sibling can do it. Because each is intertwined with the others, sometimes it is difficult to separate them. Even though this book deals mostly with anxiety, the second ugly sibling, one must not underestimate the mighty other two—stress and depression.

Because each is destructive, one must use the process of recovery and healing when confronted by the three. Why are they labeled "ugly"?—because they seek to rob a person of life's joys, happiness, and freedom in life.

We can face each sibling toe-to-toe and emerge triumphant, unbeaten, and successful. We each have the inner power which can cause the ugly siblings to retreat or to remain at-bay.